In Service

A Guide for Military Personnel and Those Who Support Them

Franklin Wesley Jr

Dedication

This book is dedicated to multiple audiences, starting with young people unsure of the direction they want to take in life.

To the recruiters, may this book serve you well.

To the families of our servicemen and women, you are the backbone of our soldiers.

To my younger self, thank you for not giving up.

This book is also dedicated to my family and friends.

And, to every service member in all military branches and to everyone who truly understands that freedom is not free - this book is for you.

Acknowledgment

Learning is a fundamental process and so, I'm grateful to everyone I've learned from. Teaching is a skill and so, I deeply appreciate those who took the time to teach me.

I want to thank everyone involved in the development and production of this book; teamwork truly makes the dream work.

To my parents, who are gone but never forgotten: your work ethic, dedication, and unwavering love shaped me into who I am. Without you, there would be no me.

Thank you to my family, friends, and supporters - it truly takes a village.

To my children, Dominic, Tyra, and Chance, may all your dreams come true. Remember: *do good, be good.*

To my active-duty sons, Tanner, Myles, and Greyson, I'm incredibly proud of you!

A big thank you to my surgeons, doctors, and counselors for your continued efforts with my physical and mental health. I have both good and bad days, and your support means the world.

To my old neighbor, Trish, I can't thank you enough for your ideas and creative outlook on life. And I can't forget the outstanding secretary you were to our homeowner's association - your dedication and teamwork were unmatched.

To my loving wife, thank you for your unconditional love and patience with me and for your understanding, help, and guidance. You are living proof that dreams do come true.

To all the soldiers who never made it back home, we honor you with pride, and we will always carry you in our hearts.

To every military veteran and those I personally served with, I want to express my thanks. Remember, once we are soldiers, we are always soldiers.

And last but certainly not least, to all active-duty United States service members: I want to thank you for being part of the world's biggest military force. Your willingness to serve allows us Americans to sleep a little better at night.

About the Author

Franklin Wesley is a Hartsville, S.C. native who became a disabled veteran while serving overseas in the U.S. Army. During his time in service, he was a highly motivated soldier who stepped up to every challenge. Facing the even greater challenge of adapting to civilian life with a disability, Franklin dedicated himself to continuing to serve others in various capacities. He has always had a passion for writing and a commitment to serving. By combining both passions with his experiences in and out of the military, Franklin has created a process that allows him to serve all military branches, military families, veterans, and civilians with valuable information, problem-solving insights, and inspiration through a unique strategy.

Franklin currently lives in Columbia, S.C., and remains dedicated to military communities as an advocate for veterans' rights.

Table of Contents

Introduction

Throughout the ups and downs of my life, I've worn many hats. My humble beginnings laid the foundation for the biggest decision I ever made at that time: enlisting in the U.S. Army at just 17. It wasn't until years later that I fully grasped the implications of that choice. That one decision sparked a flame that turned into a burning desire to continually serve others in some capacity or another.

Joining the military opened doors to travel the world and form connections with people who became like family. Although my career was cut short by an injury, it didn't diminish my commitment to service. The time I spent in the military instilled in me something that's hard to put into words. It's a unique experience that no human can ever take away – it's a sentiment every soldier who has served can understand.

Although my military career was shortened, my dedication to serving others has continued in many different ways. After leaving the Army, I served as a Letter Carrier with the United States Postal Service, becoming the face known as the Mailman in my neighborhood. I also took on the role of President of my Homeowner's Association, representing over 150 families. Overseas, I continued to serve military communities by delivering the Stars & Stripes newspaper to various locations. Additionally, I had the privilege of working with military families as an after-school Recreation Aid for youth services, and I served as a bartender at the officer's club, a cook at the non-commissioned officer's club and bowling alley, and as a materials handler, preparing military community spaces for new families.

In the civilian sector, I served in law enforcement, working closely with the United States Marshal Service, earning several recognition service coins for my contributions to their missions. I also served as a Residential Counselor for children and young adults undergoing treatment for psychiatric, addictive, and other behavioral health challenges.

I also served as a Department of Juvenile Justice Officer, where I provided direct supervised care for adolescents; hard work but rewarding. Another position I had the pleasure to serve in was as a Safety Associate at several public library locations, where I maintained a safe, relaxed atmosphere while assisting patrons with directions to resource areas of interest.

I've owned several businesses, including an event planning company where I organized special events tailored to individual needs and a vending business that provided affordable snacks and drinks to local businesses and community housing developments.

I've also served my family by reconnecting siblings who are without transportation or unable to drive and organizing family reunions to make sure that everyone stays connected. One of the roles I'm most proud of is being a wedding officiant, where I continue to unite couples in marriage, in which I find immense fulfillment.

Now that I'm recalling all this, it all started at the age of 17 when I made the life-changing decision to enlist in the United States Armed Forces. That decision sparked a flame that ignited a lifelong passion for service. If you've made it this far, I want to thank you for your time, and I hope this book has piqued your interest. There's much more to discover inside! I'm also deeply grateful if you've purchased this book, knowing that a portion of the proceeds will benefit military families and support various military facilities and establishments.

My enlistment into the military didn't just change my life - it gave me the ability to help change the lives of others in more ways than one. This book is a tool that allows me to uphold the promise and oath to never leave a fallen comrade behind. Through this book, I'm able to continue that mission in a new way. When I reflect on my journey, I can only imagine how much this book would have changed my own life if I had it during my younger years. It would have been a very useful guide for me, helping me navigate through challenges both before and during my military service. Without a doubt, it would have saved me time and money and helped me make better-informed decisions during those crucial moments of uncertainty.

Now, I want to share this information to help others. I feel that the beauty of this book is that it's designed to benefit a wide range of people - men, women, adolescents, professionals, and non-professionals from all walks of life. My hope is that everyone who reads it will find something they can relate to, something that will assist them in making a positive transition to the next chapter of their lives.

We often hear the phrase, "It takes a village," and in this case, it's true! For every person who enlists in the military, their families - including mothers, fathers, siblings, and close relatives- are all part of the mental well-being of their beloved service member. Military facilities and establishments are also integral to this support system. So, to my active-duty service members and their families and to non-active-duty veterans and their families, I extend my heartfelt thanks. Your willingness to serve the United States allows many of us to sleep soundly at night.

One important thing to remember is that every veteran, whether currently serving or not, never truly stops serving. When we enlist, we take a sworn oath to defend this country, and I think that oath has no expiration date. Even when our service contracts end, the commitment to that oath remains a constant in our lives. This is why so many veterans continue to serve in different capacities, trading one uniform for another. Because once a soldier, always a soldier!

Chapter 1: History of the Military

The structure of today's government has evolved greatly from its origins in the 1700s. One of the earliest and most critical extensions of the government was the creation of the Continental Army on June 14, 1775, by the Second Continental Congress. This force, not yet known as the United States Army, was led by the elected Commander-in-Chief, George Washington. Under his leadership, the Continental Army fought against the forces of Great Britain, ultimately leading the 13 American colonies to victory and independence.

Since gaining independence from Great Britain, the United States has faced numerous conflicts, including 12 major wars involving both internal struggles and battles against foreign powers. As the oldest military branch, the United States Army has played an instrumental role in the development of America. Established on June 14, 1775, the Army was instrumental in America's growth, even before the Declaration of Independence was drafted over a year later.

Another key military branch, the United States Marine Corps, was founded on November 10, 1775, by Captain Samuel Nicholas in Philadelphia, Pennsylvania, though its headquarters is now in Arlington, Virginia. Similarly, the United States Navy, initially formed as the Continental Navy by General George Washington in 1775, was officially established by Congress in April 1798.

The United States Air Force came much later, officially established on September 18, 1947, though its roots can be traced back to the U.S. Army Signal Corps' Aeronautical Division, formed in 1907. The United States Coast Guard, founded by Alexander Hamilton on January 28, 1915, also has earlier roots, dating back to the signing of the Tariff Act by George Washington on August 4, 1790. This act was designed to enforce trade laws and prevent smuggling, laying the groundwork for the Coast Guard's mission.

Historically, only one person has served in every branch of the United States Armed Forces prior to 2019: Kenneth Wayne Graham. A native of San Antonio, Texas, Kenneth began his military career at 18 by joining the

United States Navy. He remains the only person in history to have served in every branch of the U.S. military. Born in May 1947, Kenneth passed away in December 2014 at the age of 67.

In December 2019, a newly formed military branch, the United States Space Force, joined the ranks of the Armed Forces, further expanding the focus of U.S. military operations to include outer space alongside the traditional domains of land, sea, air, and seaports.

The United States Military undergoes extensive training drills and tests with the sole purpose of being ready for war. This preparation keeps our military strong and capable of inflicting significant damage on enemies, both near and far. In the event of war, casualties are inevitable, and sadly, this often includes civilians. This is why war is always a last resort, pursued only after all efforts at communication have failed.

In our own lives, we've made decisions we later regret, often wishing for a chance to undo past mistakes. However, these choices shape us into the individuals we are today. War, too, has this dual nature. The ugly side of war is undeniable, with innocent people historically targeted, both directly and indirectly. Some difficult decisions made by military leadership in the past contributed to such tragedies. Since then, the U.S. Government has sought to make amends for the devastating aftermath of those decisions, offering reparations and special adjustments to victims of conflicts and past wars.

Over the past 400 years, wars have played a significant role in shaping the United States. Some of the major wars in which our military has fought include the Indian Wars (1609-1924), the American Revolutionary War (1775-1783), the War of 1812 (1812-1815), the Mexican-American War (1846-1848), the Civil War (1861-1865), the Spanish-American War (April 21, 1898 - December 10, 1898), World War I (1914-1918), World War II (1939-1945), the Korean War (1950-1953), the Vietnam War (1955-1975), the Persian Gulf War (1990-1991), and the War on Terror, which included the Afghanistan War (2001-2021) and the Iraq War (2003-2011).

Chapter 2: The Military Family

Every person who serves in the United States military faces the same daunting hurdle: leaving behind their immediate family, friends, and the life they've always known. However, take comfort in knowing that you will become part of an even larger family, one where some members may grow closer to you than even your biological relatives. By joining the military, you'll be entering the ranks of those who served in the past, those who serve now, and those who will serve in the future. Some of these connections will blossom into lifelong friendships, but the family bond will always remain in the hearts of all who join. Pretty cool, huh?

Another important thing to note is that this military family spans the globe. As you start connecting with other servicemen and women, you'll find that they come from all walks of life. Our United States military forces serve on various missions worldwide, and as service members, we must remember that everyone gives something - some give a lot, and some give their all. Let us never forget those soldiers who never made it home. We may not know them all, but as Americans, we owe them all our gratitude and respect.

For the military family bond to thrive, several factors must come into play. The most important, in my opinion, is the willingness of each individual to give their all for people they don't know and may never meet. When like-minded individuals come together with this shared commitment, they create a united force. From that standpoint, whatever the mission, our military will always do whatever it takes to accomplish it.

The traditional professionalism displayed by soldiers stems from core values passed down through the years. By becoming a soldier, a person becomes part of a legacy that stretches back more than 235 years. When you are placed with like-minded individuals who share the same commitment to helping those who can't help themselves, a natural bond of fellowship forms. This shared purpose creates a deep connection, compelling you to trust your fellow servicemen and women with your life. These people don't just have your back - they have your front and sides as well.

When enlisted, you go through the struggles of intense military training together, where teamwork is essential, and you learn to rely on one another in most situations. War-like simulation exercises prepare each individual for the ultimate challenge of real combat, revealing both your strengths and weaknesses. As you progress, you'll grow to understand just how important your military family is.

After successfully completing basic combat training, soldiers move on to specialized job training. This phase builds on the discipline, values, and skills learned during basic training, preparing soldiers to excel in their chosen fields, whether in combat or support roles, through hands-on training and field instruction.

As it's said, once a soldier, always a soldier!

Chapter 3: Decisions

Are you thinking of joining the military? If yes, well, this book will provide you with some incentives, ideas, structure, guidelines, and fundamentals to help you along the way. Not only will it give you a head start, but it can also serve as a tool to help you navigate your military service from start to finish.

Being a soldier will strengthen you physically, mentally, and emotionally. The military offers a wide variety of opportunities, whether you want to continue your education, travel the world, or pursue a career that is both adventurous and meaningful.

If you're still in high school and unsure of what you want to do after graduation, keep reading. If you have the chance to take JROTC or ROTC in high school, do so as soon as you can - even if you don't ultimately join the military. That training alone will build leadership skills that will benefit you in whatever direction you choose to go. Plus, joining JROTC or ROTC will give you a jump start over your peers if you decide to join the military.

Maybe you're considering going to college, or perhaps

you're thinking about jumping straight into the workforce. Hold that thought, and let us explore some scenarios.

Scenario 1:

You decide to attend college after high school. Now, you need to determine if you want to pursue a 2-year, 4-year, or longer program and whether you'll attend a college in your city or somewhere else. If you choose a college outside your city, you'll need to figure out transportation and how you'll get around once you're there. If you have your own vehicle, you'll have to manage repairs and maintenance.

Ideally, you'll have a plan for covering your college expenses, but keep in mind that you must maintain passing grades. Failing a course may require you to pay for it again, and if you receive grants, barely passing won't suffice - you might need to maintain a certain GPA to keep your funding. Additionally, with food costs rising, you may need a part-time job, which could complicate your studies. Focus on maintaining good grades, as higher grades could be the key to landing a position over other candidates.

Remember, if you plan on taking out student loans for college, you'll need to pay them back. Even if you finish college with loans and manage to land a job in your field, you'll start your career thousands of dollars in debt. Often, completing college provides the education but lacks the work experience, so you may begin in an entry-level position with a salary lower than expected.

Scenario 2:

If you choose to enter the workforce immediately after high school, whether working for an individual or a company, be aware that without specialized education and with minimal work experience, your job options and pay will likely be limited. Most entry-level positions will offer minimum wage or slightly above, which currently ranges from $7 to $11 per hour, depending on where you live.

If you're fortunate, you might find a job paying $14 to $16 an hour. However, with rising living costs, many people still struggle to make ends meet. This scenario has at least one advantage over the college route: you won't have the burden of student loan debt, which can take years to repay. On the downside, you may have to take on physically demanding jobs with long hours, which can take a toll on your quality of life. As you age, you'll come to realize just how important maintaining your physical health is.

Scenario 3:

If you become a parent before finishing high school, whether you're a young woman or a man, life can quickly become very challenging. As a young father, you'll want to provide for your child, and if you're a new mother, your options may be more limited. In such cases, joining the military can be a beneficial choice. It offers a stable career with immediate benefits and opportunities for education. The military provides training in various fields such as electrician, plumber, nurse, scientist, doctor, firefighter, and even language translator. The long-term rewards of military service often outweigh the short-term sacrifices you will have to make.

Scenario 4:

While it may be highly unlikely, starting a business right after high school is not impossible. There's a saying that if you can make a living doing what you love, you'll never work a day in your life. While this sounds appealing, it's not entirely true. Like most things in life, owning a business has its pros and cons. It comes with peaks and valleys and certainly involves high levels of stress. The responsibilities of running a business include but are not limited to managing bills, paying staff, making sure inspections are up to date, tracking inventory and overhead, maintaining accurate accounting, and keeping customers satisfied. Although owning a business can be very rewarding, it may take years to become well-established. If you choose this path, my advice is to hang in there! Continue learning, grow your business, and always look for the bright light at the end of the tunnel.

These scenarios are not guaranteed to happen exactly as described, but I can assure you that they are quite common and continue to occur frequently. The information in this book is not a one-size-fits-all solution, but it will be helpful and applicable to many. As young adults, you will make mistakes and may need to start over in various aspects of your life.

One scenario that I believe covers all your bases is enlisting as a full-time soldier in the United States military. Any branch will do. The age requirement is quite flexible, with most branches accepting enlistees up to 30 years of age and as young as 17. However, earlier enlistment is always advantageous. If full-time service isn't an option you're considering, you can join part-time by enlisting in the military reserves. This path involves basic training and schooling to learn your military specialty. Once you complete these initial requirements, you will return home and be required to report for duty one weekend a month and approximately two full weeks each year.

This arrangement allows you to work locally and possibly take college courses while figuring out your future direction. A benefit of the reserves is that you can receive military funding for college courses while working locally and serving part-time. This opportunity provides the time you need to decide whether or not you want to commit to full-time military service. Additionally, joining the reserves or the National Guard can open the door to becoming a military officer if you achieve the necessary college credentials. The National Guard offers similar benefits to the reserves but with additional perks and incentives.

This book serves as a resource that offers information

I wish I had when I was in high school and during my full-time military service. It can save you time and money, provide education to make informed decisions, and offer tools to advance your career quickly. While it would have saved me a lot of wasted time and money, it now serves as a step-by-step guide with multiple options for whatever path you choose.

Chapter 4: Relationships

Throughout our lives, we all experience a variety of relationships. Regardless of the connection, it is the quality that determines the depth of those relationships. Many will come and go, so understanding the different levels, types, and categories you place them in depends on their quality. Some may find this concept difficult to grasp, but by keeping it simple, you can gain a clearer understanding.

This concept can be useful for everyone, but especially valuable for civilians entering the military, as well as the people connected to them. It can sometimes be a touchy subject, depending on the situation or the current status of the people you're connected to. That being said, not only will your relationship dynamics change, but some relationships will also end. Your relationships with relatives will shift because you won't be able to give or receive the same level of quality time you once had with them.

Remember, relationships can be demanding, and your full attention must now focus on your military commitment. Everything else becomes secondary, as, in my opinion, the military mission takes priority. If you have a girlfriend or boyfriend before joining the military, it might be wise to mutually end the relationship. It could even be beneficial, as you must understand that you will be gone for weeks, months, or, in some cases, more than a year. A lot can - and will - happen during these periods of separation, so it's important to keep an open mind. Remember, life happens to us all.

If you're married, perhaps with a child or two before joining the military, this might be one of the hardest challenges you'll face. The first time being away from your loved ones will be the toughest military challenge for most, and although it won't be the last, it will have a great mental impact.

While you and your family might still be adjusting to military life, they, too, will face mental challenges. They'll need to prepare for being uprooted from the life they've known, which includes separation from school, family, friends, and their regular lifestyle - just a few of the challenges they will encounter. You'll also need to prepare your family for the move to wherever your new duty assignment takes you. If this is after basic training and your military occupational specialty (MOS) training, classification training, or group training, understand that this is just the beginning. Chances are, there might be many more moves throughout your military career.

Now, imagine the mental strength required if you and your family receive an overseas assignment. I remember my first overseas duty assignment, a two-year tour in Fürth, Germany. I had so many mixed emotions, mostly fear. I feared the unknown and being so far away from my family. At the time, I was only 18 with little to no travel experience, so going to another country felt like the ultimate challenge.

On the bright side, I fell in love with Germany! I made new friends, some of whom have become like family, and formed new relationships, and so you might too. It's important to maintain good relationships with people who bring out the best in you and truly have your best interests at heart. Your military relationships with fellow servicemen are just as important, if not more so.

You might go through so much together, including experiences that can impact your life forever.

Positive relationships can help in shaping and molding your personality in many ways. Always remember the importance of giving back and investing in others. Once a soldier, always a soldier!

Chapter 5: The Military Oath

The military oath states as follows:

"I (state your name) do solemnly swear that I will support and defend the Constitution of the United States against all enemies, foreign and domestic; that I will bear true faith and allegiance to the same; and that I will obey the orders of the President of the United States, and the orders of the officers appointed..."

These words become ingrained in the hearts of many Veterans for life, which represents a set of values most continue to honor.

The principles and discipline taught in the military become a tradition, reinforced by the training, skills, and knowledge each service member absorbs. You may have heard the phrase "Once a soldier, always a soldier" before reading this book, and you'll see me use it throughout this writing. We service members often apply what we learned during our time in the military in our daily lives. It's something we never forget, at least in my case. Additionally, the core standard of the military is that we never leave a fallen soldier behind.

As soldiers, we understand that freedom is truly not free. We know that sacrifices must be made daily, not just to achieve freedom but to preserve it. Our sworn military oath is one of those sacrifices. Soldiers are the patriots who hold the line of freedom, willing to make the ultimate sacrifice to protect it. This is often a lifelong commitment that extends beyond active duty. That core value is passed down through the households of many Veterans who have served our country, creating possibilities and opening doors that might otherwise remain closed.

With your Veteran status comes the title of being called a 'Veteran.' To selflessly give yourself for the sake of others is an act of bravery. Having the courage to protect the safety and freedoms of people you will never meet, even at the risk of your own life, is a great challenge. And this phenomenon will likely remain with you for the rest of your life.

As Veterans, many of us continue to serve others in some capacity. Once a soldier, ALWAYS a soldier!

Chapter 6: Basic Training

Basic training is many things. It's an introduction to the structured military way of life that systematically transforms civilians into soldiers, with a focus on weapons training and hand-to-hand combat. Each trainee is equipped with the fundamental tools necessary to master this training. Along with these tools, each person receives a step-by-step set of instructions that initiates the transformation of both mind and body. This transformation is key to helping them achieve their goal: becoming a United States Military Soldier.

Prepare to be stripped of everything you think you know and filled with what you need to know, according to military standards. Depending on the branch of service, basic training typically lasts between 11 and 13 weeks. It might undoubtedly be one of the toughest challenges you will ever face. Not everyone will make it through but fear not - most will.

During training, trainees will face their fears and learn to work as a team, helping one another become emotionally, mentally, and morally resilient throughout their transformation. Can you imagine yourself being placed with a group of strangers for months, all going through the same rigorous physical, verbal, and mental trials? Well, that is what this might be like. Gradually, your mind will adapt, forcing you to develop a level of mental toughness. As you progress through drills, tests, and repetitive training, you'll gain confidence. The more proficient you become in learning new skills, the more that confidence will grow. Many lessons learned here will stay with you for life.

Then comes the physical aspect of training. You'll be challenged daily with good old-fashioned PT (physical training). We could all use a bit of that, right? Don't worry, your body will respond and get stronger. But the mental challenge will be harder to overcome due to the deep emotional ties you have. Being away from family, friends, and life as you've known it will likely take its toll. This will get easier as you build connections and bond with your fellow service members.

My advice to you is to keep an open mind. Remember, it's always about the mission. Those who successfully complete the training will emerge as well-trained, disciplined, physically fit, and highly motivated soldiers who understand the importance of teamwork and the mission at hand.

Congratulations, SOLDIERS! Job well done! Once a soldier, always a soldier.

Here is another piece of advice to give you a head start before joining: start doing sit-ups, push-ups, jumping jacks, and jogging about four weeks before you go to basic training. Also, try getting to bed between 8 p.m. and 9 p.m. You'll thank me later.

Disclaimer: *I am not a professional. This is based on my opinion and experience. Consult with a physician before beginning any strenuous exercise.*

Chapter 7: Military School

In my opinion, one of the greatest advantages of the military is the many opportunities to learn while getting paid. "Learn as much as you can, as often as you can" is advice I wish someone had given me during my time in the service. The military not only trains you but also equips you with the skillset for your specific military specialty. It's like on-the-job training, but you're also getting a full paycheck, meals, and housing. Take full advantage of these perks to learn as much as possible.

During your military career, there will be several opportunities to take college courses, which I highly recommend. This education will deepen your knowledge within your field and sharpen your skillset, which might put you in a better position for promotion. It will also give you an edge if and when you decide to transition into the civilian workforce. The great thing is that you can go at your own pace, taking one class at a time if needed. This benefit, along with others offered while actively serving, boosts your military career and provides advantages for the future.

This extra education can benefit you in various aspects of your profession, from the physical and human resources sides to management roles. It's a great way to enhance your life during and after your military service. These opportunities alone make joining the military right after high school a compelling option compared to heading straight to college. Both paths have their pros and cons, but I think that the military allows you to "be all that you can be" - and more.

There are many fields of study to choose from, and new military programs are constantly being introduced to help keep America strong and safe. With over 100 career options in the military, you'll have the chance to do just that. As technology evolves, the military stays ahead through education and testing. Some educational opportunities may even take you to different cities or other countries.

You'll receive specialized, quality training from highly skilled professionals in your chosen field. As your understanding and knowledge grow, you'll not only advance in your career but also step into leadership roles, guiding and teaching others. The skills, knowledge, and education you gain will likely last a lifetime.

Once a soldier, ALWAYS a soldier!

Chapter 8: Military Perks

While many civilian jobs offer their employees a two-week paid vacation, as an active-duty soldier, you receive twice that amount in fully paid vacation days each year. Joining the military not only leaves a lasting impact on your immediate family's history, but you also become a part of your country's history. This service is often met with gratitude and thanks from many people of your country, both during and after your time in uniform. You'll also receive various perks for your services to the nation, which I'll elaborate on shortly.

These perks are more common while in uniform but are often extended when you're out of uniform, especially when you display your military affiliation. Wearing the uniform is a direct representation of the United States, but there are many veterans who, even though they no longer wear the uniform, are still willing to serve their country. These are the veterans who continue to live by their sworn military oath. I feel that the saying 'Once a soldier, always a soldier' is fitting here. When you wear your uniform, consider yourself an ambassador representing your branch of service wherever you go. When you're out of uniform, you still remain an important link in the chain of US military branches.

To put this in simpler terms, think back to when you first learned to ride a bicycle. Every bicycle has a chain, and every link in that chain is important. If a link is missing, the chain breaks and the rider can no longer pedal. That's how important and valuable you are to the military once you enroll. After you have served your country - and especially while you are serving - you might gain respect and appreciation from your country's people that you know and many you don't.

In recognition of your service, your country offers a variety of perks and benefits. These include, but are not limited to, discounts on clothing, meals, hotel stays, travel, home purchases, and home repairs. Many of these perks are available not just nationwide but internationally as well. Some of these benefits also extend to your family members. For example, they may enjoy paid school tuition and even priority employment opportunities, all because you're in the US military.

Moreover, many companies in our country give

preference to veterans when hiring. As mentioned earlier, the perks you'll receive due to your service will come in handy for the rest of your life.

I thank you for your service!

Chapter 9: Duty Stations

Congratulations on becoming a world traveler - compliments of the United States government! Changing duty stations is usually an undervalued benefit that some service members don't fully appreciate until later in life. For some, it's a dreaded time, especially for soldiers with families, as it can be quite stressful. Regardless of how you feel about it, as a soldier, it's the time when you have to pack up and leave behind familiar surroundings. Adding a family to the mix can make the clearing process even more tough, as there are numerous out-processing checkpoints to navigate.

These tasks include cleaning and returning various equipment, cleaning your room, stripping your bed, turning in your weapon, transferring your kids from one school to another, cleaning your temporary housing unit, making sure your household items are packed and ready for shipment, and returning all keys issued to you. These are just a few of the responsibilities you must handle before heading to your new duty station.

This change in duty station will take you to new places

where you'll experience different ways of life in unacquainted locations. Most of the time, this will be a new city, but occasionally, it might be an assignment in another country. Think of it as having something (your military specialty) that's needed, and the new duty station is where you deliver your expertise. It's not just a job but I think of it more like an adventure.

The longer you stay in the military, the more opportunities you'll have to experience different places, cultures, and regions. Each new duty station provides you with memories that will last a lifetime. Many of these experiences will be shared with others, and some will turn into stories you may one day tell your grandchildren. But despite everything, I think one thing is for sure: each duty station will offer different memories and unique experiences throughout your military career - all provided to you and your family by the United States government.

As you transition from a civilian to a soldier and then to a world traveler, you'll gain knowledge and experience with each new duty station transfer. Over time, you'll become an even greater asset to the military by constantly evolving - from student to teacher.

Once a soldier, ALWAYS a soldier!

Chapter 10: The Mission

One thing I feel about the military is that every day comes with its own mission. Some missions require a team effort, while others depend on individual dedication. Everyone receives their assignments and instructions to carry out their daily tasks, ranging from simple to complex, but each mission has its purpose. Remember, your service to this country is a big deal! One of the things that keeps the United States strong and enables us to remain a global superpower is our military force.

Many people of our country rely on our military, and the military, in turn, relies on its soldiers. Soldiers rely on good leadership, but more importantly, they rely on one another. Be aware of the job you've been given, and understand that every soldier's role is important.

For example, your job could be as a cook in the military, but it's that job that helps in making sure soldiers are well-fed to provide them with the energy and stamina they need each day. Your mission is to make sure there are adequate food supplies to serve nutritious meals. This means knowing how much food to order and how much you can prepare with the supplies available. As a cook, you also need to be aware of proper food storage and holding temperatures. These tasks are important and are just a few examples of why being a military cook is so important.

Similarly, you might be a mechanic, but that job is also important for the U.S. military. Mechanics make sure that military vehicles are always ready for action, whether for daily use, training exercises, or combat readiness. Part of the job involves preventative maintenance and repairs. A mechanic's mission could be as simple as changing the oil in all vehicles, which, in my opinion, is an important task as well.

This is why you should never underestimate or undervalue the significance of any job in the military. The military consists of many complex roles, but I think that all of them are important and depend on the quality of effort demonstrated by each individual service member. Remember, someone else is depending on you.

Chapter 11: Motivation

In my opinion, somewhere between your "what" and your "why" is where you will find your purpose. Once you find your purpose, motivation will follow. I think it's completely normal for your purpose, motivation, or both to change from time to time due to life's challenges. Whether you choose to retire from the military or decide not to renew your contract, always remember: your attitude determines your altitude. Let me repeat that - your attitude determines your altitude!

Not only are you part of a big family, but you're also a key member of a team. A highly motivated soldier is a valuable one. Your fellow soldiers will feed off your positive energy, and this can benefit you in unexpected ways. Your energy and attitude can open doors, create opportunities, and place you in positions you never thought possible.

When troop morale is low, it can be difficult to lift spirits, and that negativity can spread like a disease. If not addressed, it can become a serious issue. Your motivation can be the spark that impacts everyone around you.

There's a saying that smiling is contagious. If you don't believe it, try smiling at three people today, and chances are, at least two of them will smile back. I like to believe that motivation works similarly. While it takes effort, if you maintain a positive mindset, good things may follow. A truly motivated person finds positivity in each day, no matter what challenges arise. Mastering this mindset can be one of your strong traits, and it's a trait worth sharing with others.

Sometimes, to protect your motivation, you may need to distance yourself from toxic people or situations. These people may have deeper issues that require professional help, and until they get that help, they can drag others down with them. In the military, where missions can change at a moment's notice, this unpredictability can create stress for some people. Unfortunately, many of those affected by stress don't seek the help they need, fearing that they will appear weak. This burden can lead to a chain reaction of emotional struggles, which might affect other people and themselves in different ways.

Military life is full of ups and downs. At any given time, your fellow service members will face heartaches, pain, and personal challenges, which can be detrimental to the military's overall strength. This is why maintaining a positive source of motivation is so important. You can be that source and help to create an environment of motivated soldiers. This positive mindset not only benefits your military life but can lead to success in other areas of life as well.

Finally, no matter your current situation or role, you, too, can benefit from a motivated mindset.

Once a soldier, always a soldier!

Chapter 12: Accountability

Accountability is an important part of your military career, and it begins with each person. Being personally accountable means taking responsibility for your actions, learning from your mistakes, and constantly striving to improve. In the military, accountability is essential. When every soldier is accountable, the entire unit becomes stronger and more effective.

Since the 1800s, the United States has been considered a global superpower. This transformation began when the country shifted from an agricultural economy to one focused on manufacturing. By 1944, America led the world in arms production, supplying more than enough weaponry for its rapidly growing military. A nation's strength depends on the capability of its military to defend and protect against outside threats. For the military to maintain its proficiency, it must constantly adapt to both new and old technology. This mindset is instilled throughout every branch and every soldier, with a relentless focus on training and preparation.

The saying "practice makes perfect" holds true in the

military. Soldiers train tirelessly, repeating tasks until they become second nature. However, humans make mistakes, and sometimes bad decisions lead to accidents. While the military trains extensively to prepare for accidents through drills and simulations, there are no drills for poor decision-making. A single bad decision can have serious consequences, even the difference between life and death. That's why taking your training seriously and keeping your skills sharp is essential.

Accountability means being honest with yourself. Are you giving your best effort? If you're in a leadership role, directly or indirectly, ask yourself: *What do I expect from a leader? Do I deserve that type of leader? Am I living up to my own expectations?*

I remember a lesson from my high school basketball coach, that has stayed with me for over 30 years. He once said, "You don't come to basketball practice to practice." What he meant was that practice time is for running plays, perfecting defensive formations, and simulating game scenarios. The individual skills - shooting free throws, jump shots, and one-on-one drills - should be practiced on your own time. He called these the "intangibles" of the sport, the unseen but essential work.

I think that this lesson applies to military training as well. Accountability doesn't just come from the top down; it starts with each soldier. You are responsible for your own efforts and readiness. Practice the intangibles - whether it's reading, practicing skills, or physical exercise - whatever helps you stay sharp.

Be accountable to yourself and your team. The effort you put in every day will make a huge difference.

Chapter 13: Finances

In this chapter, we're going to talk about money. If I had access to this kind of resource when I joined the military, it would have saved me a lot of time and money. We're discussing *your* money and how to make it work for you. Many of us didn't learn financial literacy in school, and I certainly didn't. It took me years as an adult to understand how money works.

When I joined the military at 17, I thought saving my money and paying for everything in cash meant I didn't need credit. I was wrong. Your credit history determines how much a bank will loan you for big purchases. So, it is my personal opinion that you start using your checking account - pay your phone bill with it, for example. Banks want to see how you manage your money before they lend you any.

You might need loans for major purchases and sometimes even for smaller ones. You might need a loan for your first car, a smartphone, a stereo, a house, or even a lawnmower. You probably won't have enough money in just one or two paychecks to buy these things outright, and you don't want to spend your entire paycheck on minor purchases, either. That's where loans come in.

If your credit history shows maturity, meaning you've had your accounts for a year or two and have been paying your bills on time, you'll have a better chance of getting a loan. It's important to pay back what you borrow. If your credit goes into default, it can hurt your chances of getting loans in the future for a long time.

Don't overextend yourself by spending too much. Keep in mind that some jobs check your credit before hiring you, and your credit can also impact your chances of getting a promotion. So, the sooner you start building good credit, the better off you'll be in the long run.

Chapter 14: Illness and Injuries

Did you know that while you're actively serving, the military (often referred to as 'Uncle Sam') is responsible for your well-being? Yes, you volunteered for the military, but with that comes a comprehensive healthcare plan provided at no cost while you're serving.

Consider this: if you walk into a grocery store and slip on a wet floor, injuring yourself, you'd likely seek medical care. You might need medication or even surgery, which creates a medical history. In this case, you could sue the store for damages. In the military, things are a bit different. You don't sue, but you can submit claims for the benefits you've earned before your enlistment ends or after you leave. To save time, it's highly recommended to submit these claims *before* you exit the military. You'll need supporting documentation, which is where your medical history becomes important.

Now, let's talk about why maintaining a strong military force is so important. The military must show power and strength not only to reassure the public but also to deter enemies. As an active-duty soldier, showing any sign of weakness is often frowned upon. You're trained to be physically and mentally tough, serving alongside other well-trained soldiers. However, it's important to remember that you're human. You will get sick. You will experience minor injuries. There will be days when you don't feel your best, and that's okay.

Some days, you may just need rest. In that case, you can use one or more of the paid vacation days you've earned. But if you have any kind of injury or illness, no matter how minor, make sure to seek treatment. A minor headache today could turn into a major problem tomorrow.

Make it a priority to get all your medical records from every doctor, hospital, or clinic - whether military or civilian - as soon as possible. Keep these records safe. Consider getting a small file cabinet to store your military documents, starting with your first physical. You may want to keep your medical information separate from your non-medical information, but you can always cross-reference them if needed.

I can't emphasize enough how important it is to keep these records safe. They will be helpful when you need to access your medical history or make a claim in the future.

Chapter 15: Mental Health

One of the hardest things to do is admit that we are experiencing a mental crisis or breakdown, but the reality, in my opinion, is that we all face them at some point. Throughout our lives, we will encounter crises - some more frequently than others. Contrary to popular belief, men are just as vulnerable to mental breakdowns as women. In a society where men are often expected to be leaders and risk-takers, it takes real strength and courage to ask for help, let alone admit to having a mental crisis.

If you're struggling, please seek help! But let's not think of getting help as something bad or shameful. Let's focus on the word *crisis* for a moment. There are many things that can trigger a crisis, whether it's a single event or a series of events that overwhelm the brain's ability to cope. Our brain is a complex organ and is responsible for regulating our body, controlling things like motor skills, breathing, emotions, and vision to memory, touch, and thoughts, to name a few.

Think of the brain like a computer, and think of a crisis as a computer glitch. Sometimes, fixing that glitch is as simple as restarting or resetting the system. Similarly, a crisis can sometimes be resolved with a simple action. Crises can vary in nature. Some, like a car accident, can happen in the blink of an eye, while others build up over time, becoming more complex.

For example, a car accident might lead to a deeper mental crisis, especially if significant damage was caused. The sickness of a loved one can trigger feelings of helplessness or despair, which can result in a mental crisis. The sooner you would begin addressing the crisis, the less likely it might be to spiral into something more complicated.

Military personnel are particularly at high risk due to the nature of their lifestyle, which often brings immense pressure and stress. Whether you're in the military or not, talk to someone - either a professional or someone you trust. Sometimes, your 'reset' can be as simple as gaining a new perspective or hearing a different point of view.

The first step, recognizing that you're facing a mental health issue you can't shake, is difficult. The next step, realizing that you need to talk to someone, can be just as hard. Remember, you won't have all the answers, and you don't have to face your crisis alone. Often, you'll feel a sense of relief after opening up for the first time, and from there, it becomes easier to talk, and you may find yourself wanting to do it more.

I want to emphasize again that a crisis can be triggered by many things. For example, if you won a million dollars today, this life-changing event could still trigger a crisis. How would you spend the money? What would you do first? How would you handle the pressure of people constantly asking for a share? These stressors can create a mental health strain as your brain is pulled in multiple directions. This is why you should be very careful while going through big changes in life. For example, couples are often encouraged to seek marriage counseling before tying the knot. A counselor will ask questions about scenarios you may not even think of, especially when you're filled with love and excitement in the moment.

In my opinion, all military personnel, active or not, should receive some form of counseling, regardless of whether they've seen combat. This support should extend to their families as well. Though it isn't discussed enough, the military suicide rate is alarmingly high, and in my opinion, even one veteran suicide is too many. Your mental health should always be a top priority. There are various mental health services available for military personnel, veterans, and their families. Some common services include treatment for depression, substance abuse, and post-traumatic stress disorder (PTSD). There are also specialized programs for specific groups, such as women, homeless veterans, and older veterans.

No human knows *you* better than you do. If you feel something is off with yourself or someone you know, speak up. Remember, the life you save could very well be your own.

Chapter 16: Prayer

For individuals who are religious, believers or non-believers, I think that there is one thing we can be certain of. In one way or another, we face difficult times as well as hardships. How we handle these situational life experiences is important. Some people will tell you to always pray before these situations or while going through these tough situations. Though prayer, or the act of praying, is often considered to be a religious concept, in my personal opinion, it can be practiced individually or in groups of people.

With the growth of our country and military, we've seen increased cultural diversity and acceptance of different belief systems. This diversity has seen a greater range of religious practices and perspectives. Our military is made up of individuals from various backgrounds, all of whom are protected by the U.S. Declaration of Independence, which states that all men are created equal. These same individuals have sworn an oath to support and defend the U.S. Constitution, to obey the orders of the President, and to follow the commands of appointed officers. At times, there may be conflicts between personal beliefs and the duty to follow orders. During these challenging moments, many people turn to their faith for the courage to move forward with difficult tasks. Others pray for strength and guidance in the face of adversity.

I pray that you be guided to the right path and that you stay strong during times of strife and grief. I pray that the storms we face be short and swift. It is my prayer that we always have the courage and strength to fight another day. I pray that we feel love and warmth throughout the remainder of our days. Amen.

Chapter 17: Retention In The Military

The United States military stands as one of the strongest instruments of freedom for our nation. We are considered to be one of the top super-powered countries protecting all within our borders while providing assistance to our allies. A nation's strength is often reflected by its military force, and to maintain that strength, we need men and women to fill the ranks of every military branch.

For the soldiers currently enlisted, their growing military experience is crucial in continuing to serve as a beacon of freedom for our United States and its allies. Retaining seasoned soldiers ensures that new recruits are better prepared for duty, benefiting from the guidance of those who have come before them. We need these experienced soldiers to re-enlist before their service contracts end, and the decision to stay often depends on how they feel they've been treated throughout their careers.

As a leader, it is essential to coach with skill and lead with courage. Your leadership is the glue that binds results, accountability, and commitment together. No matter how long you serve or how far you rise through the ranks, remember that while in U.S. military uniform, you represent all United States soldiers. Each service member has their own role, and potential new recruits look up to the positive examples set by those in leadership roles.

For these reasons, it's imperative that you display positive military representation and lead by example. When in uniform, you set the stage for those who may aspire to follow in your footsteps. You could be the one to inspire current soldiers to continue serving by re-enlisting. I think that the phrase "each one, teach one; each one, reach one" perfectly illustrates this. If you teach one soldier, that soldier will likely pass on that knowledge to another. Now imagine if you not only teach but also reach multiple soldiers every day. The impact of your leadership can ripple through the ranks, encouraging and boosting the morale of others who look to you as a role model.

Life happens to us all. There will be ups and downs, heartaches, disappointments, and pain. As U.S. service members, it's vital to remember that the mission always comes first. But at the end of the day, we're all human. As you advance in your career and take on more responsibilities, remember to take care of your soldiers. Show empathy and understand that military retention is greatly influenced by how soldiers are treated by their immediate chain of command.

Never forget: life happens to us all.

Chapter 18: Retirement Preparation

Now I think this is the fun part, and congratulations! Your time in service is coming to an end, and you can finally see the finish line. However, there are a few things to consider, so don't wait until you reach that finish line to prepare. Whether you've served for 6, 20, or even 25 years, there are steps you'll need to take to get ready for life after the military. Ideally, I think you should start preparing about a year out, but earlier is better. The key is to give yourself plenty of time to 'shop around,' so to speak.

Start by researching the job market in areas where you might want to live. A well-written, professional resume that includes at least 10 years of work history would be good, assuming you have that much experience. It may even be worth hiring a professional resume writer to help you stand out. Depending on your military role, you might be able to transfer your skills directly to the civilian workforce. If you decide to continue your education instead, that's an option, too. The good news is you'll have a few different paths to choose from. The most important thing, in my opinion, is preparing well in advance of leaving the military.

Make a list of potential places to live, and start by examining the job markets in those areas. Compare the cost of living and research average salaries and housing prices in each location. Also, I think you would definitely want to know which areas have the highest and lowest tax rates.

Before you leave the military, you'll need to attend a few important appointments, such as your exit dental and physical exams. Make sure you don't miss these! Also, reach out to people in the civilian sector who work in fields that interest you. They can offer insight into what it's like to work in that area and what qualifications are needed. Be sure to ask about benefits, like sick leave, vacation days, retirement plans, etc.

Remember, as I'm writing this, the official retirement age is currently 62-65, so if you retire from the military with 20 years or more, you may have the opportunity to retire a second time from the civilian sector. When you reach 62-65, you can retire for good - or keep working if you choose.

There's one more important thing to understand: transitioning from the structured military lifestyle to civilian life can be a big adjustment. The longer you've been in the military, the more challenging this transition might be. It can feel like a culture shock, and for some, it may lead to depression. I think the sooner you find something to keep yourself busy, the better. Volunteering for positive causes might be fulfilling, and you can do it as often as you like. You might also want to pick up a new hobby or join a group or organization with others who share similar interests. Thanks for serving, and remember, once a soldier, ALWAYS a soldier!

Chapter 19: Veterans Affairs (VA)

The Veterans Affairs office, also known as the Veterans Administration - or sometimes the Veterans Assistance Program, depending on who you ask - is often referred to simply as the VA. It is an executive branch department of the federal government, primarily known for providing healthcare benefits to eligible military veterans at VA medical centers and outpatient clinics across the country. The VA has been providing services to veterans since the 19th century. However, there are other benefits provided by the VA that many eligible veterans don't know about. These benefits are not limited to veterans; eligible family members can also receive various services.

After being medically discharged from the military, I didn't learn about the full range of benefits available through the VA until many years later. The information I received came in bits and pieces from other veterans. Each shared different benefits they had learned about.

Eventually, I decided to visit my local VA office to find out what the VA was all about. That day, I left with regret, wishing I had known about these benefits much earlier. I felt let down in so many ways by my military chain of command, which didn't inform me of these opportunities - one of the reasons I wrote this book.

Once I learned about the various benefits and services offered by the VA, I started seeking out what suited me best at the time. Although veteran healthcare services are a primary gateway to VA benefits, they are far from the only way to access the resources available.

One of the most important documents a U.S. veteran can have is a DD214, which serves as documented proof of military service and details the conditions of discharge. This, along with other essential paperwork, is key to unlocking a wide range of VA programs. Depending on what you're applying for, remember that many other veterans are also waiting for their benefits requests to be processed. The more documentation you have ready to submit with your request, the faster the process may go, as it saves the VA time from having to look for the information. This could mean the difference between waiting months or even years for your claim to be approved.

If your request is denied due to lack of proper evidence, don't get discouraged. There are more than 100 organizations that serve veterans, many of which offer their services free of charge. Some of these organizations work directly within the VA that help veterans submit claims and appeals and make sure that all necessary documents are included. Disabled American Veterans, known as the DAV, is the organization that helped me the most. Other organizations include The American Legion, Veterans of Foreign Wars (VFW), Paralyzed Veterans of America, and AMVETS (American Veterans), just to name a few.

Chapter 20: Life After The Military

From my experience, life after the military can be exciting but also a little intimidating for some. How you feel might largely depend on how long you have served. Regardless of your length of service, I think that everyone is affected in some way. Just remember the path you traveled to get here. I find it admirable to have the bravery to face and bear danger or pain and equally commendable to have the courage to confront negative situations involving both. Possessing both bravery and courage is exceptional, and the ability to do what others can't can sometimes be rewarding.

After serving your country, you have the option to relax or take your life in a new direction. Many of us continue to serve in other capacities, but whether you retire or choose not to re-enlist after your contract ends, this marks the beginning of a new chapter. Retirement from the military gives you the opportunity to focus on hobbies or even use your skills to start a business. You may want to transfer your military skills into a civilian workforce position. Whatever path you choose after the military, I think it's important to find something that brings you both peace and fulfillment. Otherwise, you might find yourself sinking into depression or feeling unfulfilled.

In military life, we are used to having a mission, so transitioning to civilian life might take some adjustment. There are many military support groups you can connect with. These groups offer opportunities for veterans to bond with others who share similar experiences.

As I said before, volunteering toward positive causes might help as well as it gives you the flexibility to contribute just a few hours a week, and there are plenty of opportunities in different organizations. Many places offer ways to give back, allowing you to continue serving in a different capacity. As I previously stated, many of us continue to serve in some form.

Once a soldier, always a soldier!

Chapter 21: Healing

This aspect of military service is often overlooked, but I think that it is important and should be talked about more. After leaving the military, every veteran should receive counseling to address any potential unseen mental trauma that may have occurred during active service. Simply being part of the military's structured way of life for an extended period is enough to warrant counseling, in my opinion, even if it's not provided by the military. Let's be clear: counseling is not a bad thing. I think that it should be seen as a valuable tool for support and healing.

As soldiers, we are trained, both physically and mentally, to be brave, fearless, and strong, to never surrender, and to always show courage in completing every mission. Often, soldiers remain in 'mission mode' even after the mission is over, and this can carry into civilian life after military service ends.

During military service, soldiers undergo many hours of drills, exercises, tests, combat scenarios, weapons training, and more, frequently with varying levels of intensity that challenge both the mind and body. Knowing that there's always a mission ahead, soldiers are trained to be prepared for anything, even adversity that may bring injury or death to themselves or others. Throughout our entire military careers, whether we serve for a few years or many, the focus is always on the mission. For many of us, even after our service ends, we're still mentally 'serving.'

I think that this mindset alone makes it difficult to adjust to civilian life. Veterans often continue to serve in other structured professions, but some of us never find the same sense of fulfillment that came from being an active-duty soldier. The whole civilian life navigation process after the military can be a daunting task that many Veterans don't realize just how difficult it is until they are out of the military for a little while.

Given all these factors, it's important to recognize that healing from a life of active duty takes time. Understanding this might help you, or someone you love, prepare for a smoother transition from military to civilian life. This knowledge can also lead you to self-help programs or resources that may assist you in creating a game plan before you exit the military.

That said, I personally appreciate your service to your country. As always, thank you for serving!

www.ingramcontent.com/pod-product-compliance
Lightning Source LLC
Chambersburg PA
CBHW051550120626
46551CB00013B/1458